W9-CFL-363

Roth IRA
Exploding the Myths

To Convert or Not
In 2009/2010

By
John Azodi, CPA

First Edition

1

3 1257 01895 3942

*This book is for
my brother
Massoud Azodi*

محبت

*Who made it possible
for me to come to the
United States of America
and obtain the privilege of
U.S. citizenship*

تشـكر

2

TABLE OF CONTENTS

PREFACE

*In which the author states his biases and
tells you how this book should be read*

Since 1982, I have been a certified public accountant doing
tax returns and tax planning. Then in 1994, I started helping
companies set up profit-sharing and 401(k) plans. For many
companies the purpose of setting up a retirement plan is to
pay the least amount of taxes now, and at the same time,
help employees save for retirement. When I was educating
business owners about various retirement plans (such as
401(k), 403(b), TSA, profit-sharing, money purchase,
SEP/IRA, or defined benefit), they stated that finally they
"got it." And they got it because I did not try to sell them
any investment products, I simply explained to them how
the various retirement plans work and what is involved.

Once they decided to provide the plan best suited to their
employees, at that point, I would recommend that they
work with their investment advisor if they had one, or I
would recommend one to them. I recommended working
with advisors because I felt that most employees needed to
learn some of the basics of investing. Most companies did
not use an advisor, and offered no-load funds for the 401(k)
investments. The 401(k) provider usually sends sales
people or a broker to advise the employees just once, at the
beginning. Unfortunately, the sales people were again
trying to sell the company and its employees on the
investment products rather than selling them on the benefits
of investing, which usually lead to the company having low
participation in the 401(k) plan. Consequently, the

employees who did join were on their own to choose the investment options without knowing much about investing.

At this point, I decided to educate the employees about the basics of investing and explain why they should contribute to the 401(k) plan. Employees' interest grew and so did participation in the plan because I was speaking the language that the employees understood, not sales talk. I do believe that most 401(k) plan providers should provide advisors for their plan participants. Of course, there is an additional cost for having a plan with an advisor. However, I think a plan with a **good** advisor is worth the additional cost.

Then, in 1998, when the Roth IRA was established, I talked to most of my tax clients during the tax season. I explained to them the tax benefits of starting and contributing to a Roth IRA and why they should start one. Most of them agreed and were interested in starting one. I explained that I was not licensed to open a Roth IRA for them, but recommended they go to their financial advisor or do it themselves if they were knowledgeable about investing. In cases in which clients did not have an advisor, I referred them to a couple of advisors I knew. At the end of the tax season, only two clients had set up Roth IRAs, even though more than fifty of them had shown interest in opening one. Most clients simply did not want to take the time to go see a new advisor to set up a Roth IRA even though they believed they should.

That is when I decided that I needed to provide advisory business as a service of my tax practice. By then I felt I was qualified to educate clients because I had been doing it for 401(k) plans. Because I started educating people about basic investment options, and I was not getting paid for educating them (I was being paid for doing taxes and administering retirement plans), I learned about many different investment options without being influenced by how I was paid. Obviously, after I became licensed to sell and service investments, I was compensated based on the products that I recommended to clients. Since then, I have used many types of investments with my clients. The investment world is constantly changing and I am constantly learning about new products and new tax laws. I knew I could make life a lot easier in my office by only using one or two products and fitting everybody into them (as many do), but that was not the right thing to do. Therefore, I am not going to tell you which investments you should use.

FOREWORD

What this book will do for you, and what it will not

In my 25 years of experience in the financial and tax business sector, I have found that the Roth IRA plan is a good way to invest for retirement. I am writing this book after 10 years of listening to too many of my clients questioning or declining my offer to set up a Roth IRA. This was due to the misconception that the Roth IRA is undesirable because taxes must be paid on it in advance.

I believe individuals create wealth not by how much they invest, when they invest or what they invest in, but simply by the behavior of the individuals who invest. It is the consistency of the savings that helps creates wealth.

I have noticed during my years of financial and tax advising that many individuals become financially wealthy even though they started with nothing, did not inherit a dime, did not finish college and, in some cases, did not even finish high school. I am not encouraging that because I do believe education is one of the most important investments anyone can make. Some never made more than $30,000 a year, and with that much income even managed to put their children through private colleges. Why have they created wealth? Because they are the ones who bought a $25 or $50 (it did not matter how much) bond or stock every paycheck or put that amount in a savings account. According to the *U.S. Census Bureau, Housing and Household Economic Statistics Division Last Revised: July 14, 2008*, only 8.5% of all households in the United States

9

have $500,000 or more in assets. See Appendix A to understand how much investing $50 a month over a long period would do for you. Obviously, the amount of wealth created will be different depending on the amount invested, but they still created wealth. They are among a few of American population who are considered financially independent.

I believe the Roth IRA gives our generation (after 1998) even greater incentives to create wealth than the previous generation, but only if we use the opportunities that the government is giving us via the tax-free growth of Roth IRA and the availability of systematic investing.

I am writing this book to be a simple guide, much like a recipe, for understanding the Roth IRA and its benefits. Why simple? The American public doesn't need another several hundred page financial planning book they can't remember why they picked up in the first place when they've finished it— if they ever finish it!

The following information is designed to help you implement this important step for your financial planning. Based on a study completed by American Century Investment Company, an article in the April 7, 2005 issue of *Business Wire,* reported that: "On a 10-question test taken by more than 800 investors, knowledge of some of the most basic investment concepts is poor. Only 2 percent of the investors surveyed answered all 10 questions correctly. On average, participants selected about half of the correct responses on the multiple-choice test, which was to individuals who have investments outside of a company retirement plan." Do not worry if you are not included in these minimal percentages because you are not

10

alone. I believe that the overall percentage of Americans who truly understand the Roth IRA and its benefits is similar to or even lower than the percentage reported in the study, especially with so many pundits discouraging the use of the Roth IRA. People are blinded by the tax they would have to pay up front, which results in them overlooking the many benefits of the Roth IRA.

In the following pages, I will explain the theory behind the Roth IRA, its contributions and limits, its benefits and its lingo. For those of you who are looking for a more technical explanation of the Roth IRA, this is not for you. In order to start a Roth IRA you do not need to know all the rules, just the basics. When you buy a television, do you need to find out how it works technically or do you buy it because it works?

For those who cannot contribute to a Roth IRA or do a Roth IRA conversion, this book will help you learn more about an IRA or 401(k) plan, and how to make informed decisions about investing or choosing the right advisor.

In summary:

- I will explain to those of you who qualify for the Roth IRA plan, the tax benefits of contributing to this plan.
- I will remove the myths and confusion that surround the Roth IRA plan.
- I will convince you that a Roth IRA is a great way to help accumulate wealth for retirement.
- I will change your old perceptions of an IRA as tax deductible and tax deferred. And I will explain why

11

a Roth IRA almost seems at odds with what we have been taught about an IRA.

- I will give you enough information so you can make decisions about what is important, but not so much information that you feel paralyzed when it comes to making a decision. That is why I will cover many subjects, but will try to make the explanations as simple and as brief as possible.

Section One

Demythologizing the Roth IRA

Chapter 1
What is a Retirement Plan?

The purpose of a retirement plan is to invest money during your working life so that when you retire you can use that money plus any pension or Social Security income to create a comfortable living. Congress has established some plans to help you accomplish this by allowing tax-favored treatment of these savings.

These tax-favored plans have different names, but in principal there are two types. The first type, called Qualified accounts such as 401(k) plan, 403(b) plan, TSA, 457 Plan, Simple IRA, and the Individual Retirement Account (IRA), are the ones for which you pay no income tax when the money is saved; however, you pay income tax later when it is withdrawn. For the second type, the Roth IRA, you pay tax on the money initially; and when the money is withdrawn the earnings is income tax-free.

The following pages will provide more details for each plan.

14

Chapter 2
IRA vs. Roth IRA — The Basics

The Roth IRA started in 1998 by Senator William (Bill) Victor Roth Jr. of Delaware. He wanted to help Americans save for retirement and, at the same time, make it simple. The Roth IRA is similar to a regular IRA, but with two major differences. However, before we get into the differences, I will explain the IRA in simple terms to make the comparison easier.

What is an IRA?

An IRA is a retirement account in which you deposit pre-tax money (accumulation phase). In addition, you pay no tax on any gain, reinvestment, sale, or transfer (rollover) into another IRA. It is only taxed when you start taking money out (distribution phase) after a certain age (usually after age 59½ without a paying any penalties). When you receive the distribution, you will pay tax based on your tax bracket at that time. The same rules apply to many other retirement plans, with the only differences occurring during the accumulation phase being the limits and rules imposed by the IRS or individual companies. So, throughout this book, when we talk about an IRA, it has the same tax implications as if you have any other retirement plans, such as a 401(k), TSA, 403(b), pension, profit-sharing, SEP/IRA, simple IRA, solo 401(k), 457 plans, as well as some ESOP plans and defined pension plans.

This is a very simple description of what an IRA is. The IRA rules are actually very complex and cover hundreds of pages.

15

What is a Roth IRA?

Simply put, with a Roth IRA you contribute money on which you do pay income tax; in other words, it is after-tax money that you invest. Once you set up this account and contribute this money, it grows tax-deferred as long it remains in a Roth IRA. Once you are older than 59½ and have had the Roth IRA for at least 5 years, then the earnings becomes tax-free and it is called a "qualified Roth IRA." But if you take the Roth IRA out before age 59 ½, even after holding it for more than 5 years it is taxable and subject to penalty. Also, if you started the Roth IRA after you turn 59 1/2 , in order for the earning to be tax free you must hold it for at least 5 years or more .

After a Roth IRA becomes a "Qualified Roth IRA" the total distribution is tax-free since you have paid the tax on the original investment.

16

Chapter 3
Lawmakers' Intent in Creating the Roth IRA

Congress created the Roth IRA retirement plan in 1998. Why is it under-utilized by the tax clients I have seen in the past 10 years? Why is it blanketed with confusion and misunderstanding with many clients that I have come in contact with? In my opinion, the Roth IRA is an easy concept to grasp in the modern retirement investment jungle.

However, Congress did add supplementary rules and qualifications to the Roth IRA plan. In my experience, these additional qualifications come off as a "catch" to many people who begin investigating what they perceive to be the "too good to be true" aspect of this plan. And, indeed, there is a catch. I think the best way to explain it would be in the form of the following example.

If you invest $2,000 in a regular IRA, you are able to deduct that amount from your tax return for the year in which you invest it (with a certain income limit). For example, if your tax bracket is 20%, you will save $400 in taxes that year. This means that if you did not invest the $2,000 in the IRA, you would only have $1,600 to invest in a Roth IRA.

Let us see the result if you saved $1,600 (on which you had paid taxes) in a Roth IRA (for which the withdrawals would be tax-free) versus $2,000 in an IRA tax-deferred. At retirement, you would, of course, have more money with the IRA versus the Roth IRA. However, if you are in the same tax bracket (20%), after you pay the tax on the IRA

17

you end up with the same amount of money accumulated in the Roth IRA. See Table 3.1. This illustrates that if at age 20 you invested $2,000 versus $1,600, you would have the same amount of money at age 65. The percentage of earnings does not have any impact on the tax but makes a big difference on the amount of money you may have. For example, if your investment makes an average of 8% versus 4%, that is a $53,824 difference, so Congress is correct on the math. In the real world, it does not work that way, because when given the chance to save in a Roth IRA, most people save the full $2,000 (or current limit), not the after-tax amount of $1,600 as in the example.

Table 3.1: Tax-Deferred IRA vs. Tax-Free Earnings Qualified Roth IRA, with Different Growth Rate*

	IRA				Roth		
Age	AMOUNT SAVED	Earning 4.00%	Earning 8.00%	Age	AMOUNT SAVED	Earning 4.00%	Earning 8.00%
Now	2,000	2,080	2,160	Now	1,600	1,664	1,728
20	0	2,163	2,333	20	0	1,731	1,866
30	0	3,202	5,036	30	0	2,562	4,029
40	0	4,929	11,743	40	0	3,944	9,394
50	0	7,297	25,352	50	0	5,837	20,282
60	0	10,801	54,733	60	0	8,641	43,787
65	0	13,141	80,421	65	0	10,513	64,337
Tax	0	(2,628)	(16,084)	Tax	0	0	0
Net Value	0	10,513	64,337	Net Value	0	10,513	64,337

*The interest rates of 4% and 8% are for illustrative purposes only. This is not a guarantee of future interest rates or financial return. This illustration assumes deposits made at the beginning of each year. This illustration does not account for reduction for inflation.

Many opponents of the Roth IRA plan use this example to discourage those interested in this profitable retirement plan. They have also used arguments such as: "You have to

18

pay taxes on the contribution to the Roth IRA and then the rules might change and you will have to pay taxes again." "The Roth IRA – don't bother. It's too good to be true." "Well, you can only do what is certain today, which is a tax-free investment."

I believe people use these statements as an excuse for not doing anything. Even if the rules change and the earnings are no longer tax-free, you have still accumulated a portion of it tax-free.

Many of my clients who have refused to start a Roth IRA plan during the past 10 years have used an example similar to the ones above. However, in the real world, the Roth IRA does not play out as Congress planned. Usually, after I explain how the Roth IRA works, my clients invest the full $2,000 (or the limit that is available for that year) and not the after-tax amount. Therefore, they are investing the whole $2,000 not the $1,600. By investing the $400 that you would have paid in income taxes (which you would have most likely spent anyway) your investment instead could grow by an additional $16,840. Now, it is easy to see that the Roth IRA means more money in the pockets of you or your beneficiaries.

I do see a small number of individuals who only invest $50 a month (see Appendix A), or whatever they can afford to invest, after they realize the value of a Roth IRA. See Appendix B for comparisons of the potential for growth by investing $1,600 or $2,000 per year for 10 years in an IRA versus a Roth IRA.

Another major advantage of the Roth IRA pertains to the taxability of Social Security income. I could only assume that some of the opponents of the Roth IRA either do not know about this advantage or do not understand it (because of the complex tax law). What is it? Well, once you start receiving Social Security benefits (after age 62 or later) you may be required to pay income tax yearly on your Social Security, based on your total income. Currently, if the total of all your income plus half of your Social Security benefits exceeds $25,000 (if single) or $32,000 (if married filing jointly) then up to 85% of your Social Security benefits will become taxable. Let us use examples to illustrate with a summary in Table 3.2.

Example 1: Suppose that you and your spouse (age 62 and age 63) receive $26,000 in total income from pension, interest or any other income in the 2007 tax year, but not any Social Security income. Based on 2007 tax law and the use of standard deductions, your total income tax (federal and state of Missouri, for other state consult with your tax advisor) would be $952.

Example 2: It's the same scenario as Example 1, but you received $12,000 in Social Security income in the 2007 tax year. At this amount, you will not pay any income tax on the Social Security income of $12,000 ($26,000 plus one-half of Social Security income, which is $6,000, equals $32,000, less the threshold amount of $32,000 for married filing as joint [MFJ] equals zero). Based on 2007 tax law and the use of standard deductions, your total income tax

20

(federal and state of Missouri) would be the same as in Example 1, $952.

Example 3: It's the same scenario as Example 1 (you received no Social Security income). However, due to an emergency or a vacation you took $10,000 from your IRA. Based on 2007 tax law and the use of standard deductions, your total income tax (federal and state of Missouri) would be $2,797, which is an increase of $1,845 in income tax. This means the $10,000 withdrawal cost you $1,845 in both federal and state of Missouri income tax.

Example 4: It's the same scenario as Example 3, but you did receive $12,000 of Social Security income. Based on the 2007 tax law and the use of standard deductions, your total income tax (federal and state of Missouri) would be $3,802, which is an increase of $1,005 more than Example 3. In other words, the $10,000 from your IRA cost you $1,845 in taxes, same as Example 2. However, because $5,000 of Social Security income became taxable ($36,000 plus one-half of Social Security income, which is $6,000, equals $42,000 less the threshold amount of $32,000 for MFJ equals $10,000 x 50%, which equals $5,000), that cost you an additional income tax of $1,005 for both federal and state of Missouri income tax.

Example 5: It's the same scenario as Example 4, but you received the same $10,000 from your qualified Roth IRA (the 5-year holding period has been satisfied) and you did receive the $12,000 of Social Security income. Based on the 2007 tax law and the use of standard deductions, your total income tax (federal and state of Missouri) would be $952, even though you received the additional $10,000.

21

Those people who think their tax bracket will be lower after retirement may want to take note.

Example 4 only shows that you paid income tax on 50% of Social Security income. If you took another $10,000 (for a total of $20,000) from your IRA, the taxable portion of the Social Security income would increase to 85%, for a total taxable income of $10,200. At a combined federal and Missouri income tax rate of 31%, that is $2,142 in income tax just on the Social Security portion. If that income had come from a Roth IRA, then there would be no income tax on any portion of the Social Security income.

Table 3.2: Tax Comparison of Social Security Income with IRA or Qualified Roth IRA

	1	2	3	4	5
All Income	$26,000	$26,000	$26,000	$26,000	$26,000
Social Security Income	0	12,000	0	12,000	12,000
Additional IRA	0	0	10,000	10,000	0
Additional Qualified Roth IRA	0	0		0	10,000
Total Cash collected	26,000	38,000	36,000	48,000	48,000
Taxable portion of Social Security Income	0	0	0	5,000	0
Amount subject to Income ax	26,000	26,000	36,000	41,000	36,000
Federal Income tax	853	853	1,996	2,746	853
State Tax (Missouri)	99	99	801	1,056	99
Total Federal and state Income tax	$952	$952	$2,797	$3,802	$952

22

Even if you avoid these situations and don't take any money from your IRA until age 70½, after age 70½ you have no choice but to take the required minimum distribution (RMD) and pay the increase in taxes. Please refer to Chapter 7 for further discussion about RMD.

There are some technical individuals who have run all sorts of calculations and determined that if you invest the $1,600 in an IRA and then you invest the $400 tax savings in another account and make money on that you, are probably better off. Folks, this is a lot of "what ifs."

In reality, you may be among the small of the population that would do better, but in my experience, most people would spend the $400 tax savings now and have nothing to show for it when they retire. Let's work with examples based on what the majority does, not the exceptions of a few!

23

Chapter 4
Contributions and Limits

There are two ways to set up a Roth IRA. The first one is called a contributory (or regular) Roth IRA. The second is a Roth IRA conversion, which we will discuss in more detail in Chapter 5.

The contributory Roth IRA is the most common way to fund to a Roth IRA; therefore, it is common for people to say Roth IRA without referring to the contributory portion of the name. This is how you contribute if you are working and earning money, either as an employee or working for yourself (or as a working partner in a partnership), or if you are receiving alimony. The earnings from self-employment and wages are called earned income, whereas interest, dividend and rental income are called passive income. In order to start a Roth IRA you must have earned income. You can put money into the Roth IRA up to the limit the IRS allows on the amount you have earned. For instance, if you and your spouse together had $15,000 in earned income in 2008 or 2009 and you are 50 years old or older, you can set up a $6,000 (see Table 4.1 below for limits) Roth IRA for each of you, even if only one of you earned the $15,000. If your earned income is less than $12,000, for example, $7,000, you can set up a Roth IRA for the total of $7,000. That could be any combination, such as $3,500 for each of you, or $6,000 for one of you and $1,000 for the other.

There is no age limit for starting or continuing contributions to the Roth IRA as long as you have earned income. At age 70½, however, you are no longer able to

24

contribute to a regular IRA. So people over age 70½ who do have earned income should consider starting or continuing with their Roth IRA. The limits for a person over age 50 (any day in the tax year) are higher due to the allowance of additional contributions called "catch-up contributions." Therefore, if you turn 50 on December 31, 2008, you can use the higher limit amount for the year.

The ability to contribute to a Roth IRA is eliminated for the high-income earner. According to the IRS (for 2008), you are considered a high-income earner if you make more than $116,000 annually if single and more than $169,000 if married.

If single, your contribution of $5,000 or $6,000 (if 50 years old or older) will be reduced as your income increases from $101,000 to $116,000. Once your income is more than $116,000 you are not eligible for the Roth IRA. If married, your contribution of $5,000 or $6,000 (if 50 years old or older) will be reduced as your income increases from $159,000 to $169,000. Once your income is more than $169,000, you are not eligible for the Roth IRA.

Who Is A High Income Earner?

$116,000 $169,000

For married persons filing separately, the rules are different depending on whether you are living with your spouse or not. If you are married, but lived apart from your spouse during the entire, year then the rule for single applies (see above). However,

25

if you are married and lived with your spouse even one day, then the phase out is from zero to $10,000. That means that if your income is more than $10,000 per year, you are not eligible to contribute to a Roth IRA. The IRS implemented this stipulation to prevent married people who do not qualify (as above) from filing separately (when one has little income) to manipulate the rules.

Table 4.1 (from the Internal Revenue Service) shows the amount of contribution to a Roth IRA from inception through 2009. In 2002, Congress allowed people over 50 years of age to make an additional contribution (called a catch-up contribution). The purpose of catch-up contributions was to allow those people who have not saved enough for their retirement a chance to catch up by saving more. The amount of contribution for future years will increase based on inflation.

Table 4.1 Roth IRA Contribution Limits

Year	Under age 50	Age 50 or over
1998	$2,000	$2,000
1999	$2,000	$2,000
2000	$2,000	$2,000
2001	$2,000	$2,000
2002	$3,000	$3,500
2003	$3,000	$3,500
2004	$3,000	$3,500
2005	$4,000	$4,500
2006	$4,000	$5,000
2007	$4,000	$5,000
2008	$5,000	$6,000
2009	$5,000	$6,000
Total	$39,000	$45,000

Chapter 5
Roth IRA Conversion

The second way to have a Roth IRA is to have a Roth IRA Conversion. This is for those people who already have an IRA. You can convert all or part of your IRA to a Roth IRA; however, by doing so you are required to pay tax on the amount that is converted.

Once converted, it acts like a regular Roth IRA with the same features described in the previous chapters. If you consider doing a Roth IRA conversion, the conversion must be complete before December 31. The tax is due in the year the conversion is completed. To qualify for the conversion, your adjusted gross income (AGI), without counting the Roth IRA conversion and RMD from a regular IRA if you are over $70\frac{1}{2}$, has to be less than $100,000. Your AGI is the total of all income less certain adjustments. It is shown on the last line (37) of page one of your Form 1040 tax return. Alternatively, it is on line 21 of page one of Form 1040A.

However, the IRS is allowing everyone to convert his or her IRA into a Roth IRA in the year 2010 without the AGI limit. The best part is that you have 2 years to pay the tax on this conversion. Why? Well, Congress is giving high-income earners a chance to obtain some tax-free Roth IRA because of the phase out we discussed in Chapter 4.

You may ask, "Why should I convert my IRA into a Roth IRA and pay tax on it now? Isn't the biggest reason for investing in an IRA in the first place so that I can defer the tax for as long as possible?"

27

It is true that for many this is not the right thing to do, but there are conditions that may justify converting. I will explain some of them.

You should convert your IRA into a Roth IRA under the following conditions:

Example 1: You have created negative taxable income. You create negative taxable income when your deductions exceed your income. Let's say your negative taxable income is $9,000 and you have $100,000 in an IRA. You could convert $9,000 to a Roth IRA and pay no income tax. The earnings of converted Roth IRA will now grow tax-free. Why is this? According to the IRS rule, you have technically paid tax on the $9,000 by reporting it as income. The fact that your deductions have wiped out the tax does not matter. In the eyes of the IRS, you have paid tax on this money. The following are some of conditions that may cause you to have negative taxable income:

- You have lost your job and have been living off your savings. Therefore, you have very little income for that year.
- Near the end of the year, you realize that your itemized deductions (sum of certain deductions, discussed in more detail in Chapter 28) or the standard deduction if you don't itemize (which was $10,700 for a married person in 2007) was more than your income.
- There are many similar cases to the one above. Another example may be that you have income, but you may incur major medical expenses or have donated substantial amounts of money to charity or paid a large state tax for a prior year's income. Any

28

of these can increase your itemized deductions and thus cause negative taxable income.

Example 2: This is a point that many rental real estate owners miss. Owners of rental real estate are allowed to depreciate rental property and improvements (but not the land). Because of depreciating the property, many times they end up with a negative taxable income, while their IRA's are growing and taxable. Then, by the time they start withdrawing their IRA money, they have to pay tax on it.

Example 3: The most common circumstance I have seen for conversion from an IRA to a Roth IRA is for retired seniors between the ages of 59½ and 70½. Many live on Social Security, pensions, and/or their investments that are not taxable and have very little taxable income. Even though they have large IRAs, they are not taking money out until age 70½ when they have to start their required minimum distribution, as we will discuss in Chapter 7.

For instance, a married couple could have $18,000 income and pay no income tax at all because the IRS allows them $18,000 of deductions. Social Security is not taxable unless, if added to all other forms of income (including interest from municipal bonds, even though municipal bond interest is income tax-free) is more than $25,000 for a single person or $32,000 for married people. In this case, up to 85% of Social Security could become taxable as discussed in Chapter 3.

So, if taxable income becomes negative, it makes sense to convert. The only issue is that you have to be proactive about it. This means that you have to look at your taxes and decide whether you will have negative income before the

29

end of the year. Also, if you convert, the converted part of the IRA could cause some of your Social Security income to become taxable. You must do a "what if" calculation of your taxes before you convert. Do not guess. Don't allow your CPA or tax preparer to tell you how much you can convert without doing a mock tax return if Social Security income is involved.

There are other times when it makes sense for seniors or others to convert to a Roth IRA, even if they have to pay tax on it. Here are two such examples.

Example 4: You are in a 10% or 15% federal tax bracket currently (you have to count the state income tax percentage too if you live in a state that has income taxes) and you know that by the time you take money out of your IRA you will be in a higher tax bracket, such as 25% or higher. In this case, you may want to convert as much of your IRA as possible before your taxable income changes to the next bracket. The amount of tax you pay should come from other assets to pay the tax. If you do use the money from your IRA to pay the taxes, the conversion portion would be only the amount invested. If you are younger than $59\frac{1}{2}$ and convert, you must pay the tax from other money. If you use the money from an IRA to pay the tax, then you must pay the 10% penalty on the portion used to pay the tax in addition to the income taxes. I do not usually recommend this for someone under age $59\frac{1}{2}$ if they have to pay a penalty.

Example 5: You have a large IRA and want to leave it for your children. You know they will pay tax on it and their tax rate is higher than yours. Then it makes sense to convert. You may accomplish three things with this

30

conversion: You do not have to take a RMD from your IRA after you turn 70½. Your children can stretch a Roth IRA and receive a lifetime of tax-free earnings versus a lifetime of income that is taxable, if they use the IRS RMD table and did not take more money than the RMD tables allow. Depending on the size of your estate, you could save estate tax. (Discuss this with your CPA, estate attorney, or financial advisor with expertise in estate planning, as this would require expert advice.)

What happens if you convert your IRA into a Roth IRA and when you are preparing your income taxes you realize it is costing you too much in tax or you went over the $100,000 adjusted gross income limit? The IRS allows you to reverse the conversion without any tax consequences once per calendar year before the due date of your tax return, plus the maximum six-month extension period (whether or not the return is actually extended). This is called a Roth IRA recharacterization. For example, the deadline to recharacterize a 2007 Roth conversion was October 15, 2008.

By converting, you will be reducing your IRAs, which means, after you turn age 70½, your required minimum distribution would be less.

31

Who should convert?
-You have negative taxable income
  Loss of job
  Deductions more than income
-Some real estate owners
-Seniors living on Social Security,
pensions or nontaxable investments
-Your tax bracket is about to increase
-Your beneficiary is in a higher
tax bracket than you

Last reason to convert in 2009

Has the value of your IRA
investment gone down?

Some investments are down by more than
50% since 2007. So convert an IRA account
that has lost money now, and pay the tax on
the lower value. Then, if and when your
account recovers, the earnings are tax-free.
Of course there is still the risk that your
account could lose even as a Roth IRA, but
you are given one opportunity to change it
back to a regular IRA by the tax filing time.

Chapter 6
Emergency and Short-Term Investments vs. Long-Term Investments

I even recommend using the Roth IRA as a short-term investment, emergency money, education fund or "let's buy our first home" fund. Why would I do that? Most people do not save unless there is a tax advantage. Well, the Roth IRA has it. The reason you save as a short-term investment is because it creates the habit of saving.

Additionally, if you do need the money, you can always withdraw the principal you invested without paying any income tax. Just leave the earnings or interest. After you are over age 59½, you would not pay a dime in taxes for all the earnings if you had the Roth IRA for at least 5 years.

I also recommend setting up a Roth IRA plan for children as young as one year old if they have earned income (for example, from modeling/advertising) and for seniors over 80 years old.

If you have young children working, start a Roth IRA for them. They have the potential to accumulate tax-free earnings, while, and help them learn about investing at a very young age.

I like to tell the story of my own daughter. After she opened her first savings account and opened her first bank statement, she noticed that $1.65 had been added to her balance. She asked, "Dad, what is this?" I explained to her that it was money the bank was giving to her for letting them use her money and it is what we call interest. She

33

said, "You mean I did not have to do any work to make that? That is Awesome!" I explained that rich people stay rich because their money works for them. Imagine

that you have $100,000 invested with a bank and the bank pays you 5%; that is $5,000 that you earned each year without doing anything except taking the time to deposit it. Of course, depending on the type of investment, you might have to pay income taxes on the amount earned, but you get the picture of how your money can work for you.

I believe many hardworking Americans are paying unnecessary taxes because they are repeatedly told, "You have to be young to use the Roth IRA," or "If you are over the age of 60, you don't have time to take advantage of the Roth IRA." Since when, does "over the age of 60" mean death? I believe that our senior citizens have worked hard to get us to where we are in this great country. I think they deserve to be treated with dignity and common sense. According to the IRS 2002 Uniform Distribution Table, a senior age 70 has a life expectancy of 27.4 years, and can look forward to a fulfilling life, whether spending it with grandchildren, playing sports, traveling, working or whatever they enjoy. Therefore, with potentially another 25 years or more in retirement, they need part of their money growing and why not grow the earnings tax-free?

Chapter 7
The Four Phases of an IRA and a Roth IRA

There are four phases in IRA and Roth IRA investing. The IRA rules apply to 401(k) plans, TSA plans, 403(b) plans, profit-sharing plans, money purchase plans, 457 plans, Simple IRA plans, SEP/IRA plans, company- or union-sponsored plans, or any other tax-deferred plans that you did not pay tax on when you contributed the money. There are similar rules for both IRAs and Roth IRAs, but there are differences too. In order to better understand the benefits of the Roth IRA in these four phases, I will first explain the IRA rules and then the Roth IRA rules with a summarized comparison in Table 7.1.

IRA Rules

Phase 1: Accumulation

This is from any age until age 59½. You can contribute up to the limits set forth. Your account will grow tax-deferred. If you take money out during this phase, you will pay income tax as well as a 10% penalty (25% penalty for a Simple IRA within the first 2 years of the initial contribution) on all the earnings plus the principal that you have invested.

According to the IRS Section 72(t), the 10% penalty is waived for the following exceptions:

- You have paid medical expenses that are more than 7.5% of your adjusted gross income.

35

- The distributions are not more than the cost of your medical insurance.
- You are disabled.
- You are the beneficiary of a deceased IRA owner (if the account is set up properly).
- You are receiving distributions in the form of an annuity.
- The distributions are not more than your qualified higher education expenses.
- You use the distributions to buy, build, or rebuild a first home.
- The distribution is due to an IRS levy of the qualified plan.
- The distribution is a qualified military reservist distribution.

Phase 2: Normal Distribution

Between ages 59½ and 70½ you may take money out and pay only income tax, but no penalty. You may continue to contribute to your IRA if you qualify.

Phase 3: Required Minimum Distribution

After age 70½, you must take a distribution from all of your IRA accounts each year (whether you need the money or not). This distribution is called Required Minimum Distribution (RMD). Since 2002, The IRS requires the use of a table called the Uniform Distribution Table. This table is based on life expectancy (see Appendix C for life expectancy). For example, the year you turn age 70½, the IRS table projects you will live 27.4 years longer. Therefore, you divide the total value of all your IRAs from

36

December 31st of the prior year by the 27.4 years and that is your RMD for the current year. Of course, the life expectancy will be reduced each year after that. If the value of your account stays the same for the next year, that distribution will be higher because the fraction is larger since you are a year older and your life expectancy is one year less.

Once you are over 70½, you are no longer allowed to contribute to your IRA. However, you can contribute to a 401(k) plan or any company- or employer-sponsored plan including a self-employed plan such as a Simple IRA or SEP/IRA if you are still employed and have earned income.

Phase 4: Distribution after Death

After your death, your spouse can rollover the money into an IRA in their name and delay the RMD if he or she is under the age of 70½. Your spouse must take out the RMD if he or she is over 70½ or when he or she reaches the age of 70½. However, if your spouse is under the age of 59½, it may be advisable to leave the IRA in the name of the deceased with the spouse as the beneficiary (called a beneficiary IRA). Distribution from a beneficiary IRA is not subject to the 10% penalty for early withdrawal (under the age of 59½), but it is subject to income tax.

If the beneficiary is someone other than a spouse, it gets much more complicated. The nonspouse beneficiary would be someone such as a child or any other family member or friend. A nonspouse beneficiary has three choices:

- Take the money in a lump sum and pay income tax, but no penalty.

37

- Take it out over 5 years and pay income tax, but no penalty.
- Take lifetime income based on IRS Minimum Requirement Distribution rules (see Appendix D, Single Life Expectancy Used by Beneficiaries, according to Internal Revenue Service). This is also called a Stretch IRA (discussed in Chapter 8). As the money is withdrawn, the beneficiary is liable for income tax, but not a penalty. The payout is based on the life expectancy of the nonspouse beneficiary. The account must be registered as a beneficiary IRA. If the beneficiary dies prior to depleting the IRA, the contingent beneficiary (if one or more are listed on the account) will then be able to withdraw the remaining value of the account based on the original number of years left from the original life of the nonspouse beneficiary.

However, the nonspouse beneficiary can choose to take all the money at once and pay the income tax, but not any penalty, even if they choose one of the first two options above.

If you use the RMD, you can always take more, but cannot take less than the RMD.

If you fail to take the RMD, there will be a 50% penalty on the amount that you should have taken for that year.

If there is no beneficiary listed on the account, the balance will be paid to the estate and taxed all at once to the estate.

See I told you it is complicated!

38

If the beneficiary is a living trust, you must talk to a CPA or a tax specialist, as it could get even more complicated with the potential for a major tax liability. I would not recommend using a trust as the beneficiary because the beneficiaries lose a lot of tax benefits and flexibility.

If you think you have a trust as the beneficiary, you must seek advice from someone who is an expert concerning IRA rules, rather than any attorney or tax preparer, and do so immediately.

There are reasons for setting up living trusts, mostly for control and avoiding probate, but not as the beneficiary of an IRA.

Some attorneys who set up trusts are very knowledgeable in designing the trust documents to avoid probate or who controls the assets after you die, but many do not understand the tax complexity of IRAs. In order for the trust to be the beneficiary, it must include specific language. Based on my experience, most living trusts will fail the language requirements.

Roth IRA Rules

Phase 1: Accumulation

This is from any age until age 59½(actually there is no age limit as of now). You may contribute up to the limits (see Chapter 4). Your account will grow tax-deferred; however, the earnings will become tax-free once you pass age 59½ and you have satisfied the 5-year holding period (discussed in Phase 2).

If you take money out during this phase, you will pay income tax as well as a 10% penalty only on the earnings, but not on the principal (money that you invested).

Therefore, if you need the money, you can take the principal out and leave the earnings. These rules apply to the total contribution. For example, if you invest $10,000 into two saving accounts $5,000 each and now one is worth $11,000 and the other worth $6,000, you can take the $10,000 from one. You do not need to take the principal from each investment; there will be no income tax on the first $10,000. However, if you take $11,000, then $1,000 will be subject to income tax plus a 10% penalty.

You can have my principal but please don't take my earnings!

According to the IRS Section 72(t), the 10% penalty is waived for the following exceptions:

- You have paid medical expenses that are more than 7.5% of your adjusted gross income.
- The distributions are not more than the cost of your medical insurance.
- You are disabled.
- You are the beneficiary of a deceased IRA owner (if the account is set up properly).
- You are receiving distributions in the form of an annuity.
- The distributions are not more than your qualified higher education expenses.
- You use the distributions to buy, build, or rebuild a first home.
- The distribution is due to an IRS levy of the qualified plan.
- The distribution is a qualified military reservist distribution.

As you can see, you have more flexibility with a Roth IRA than with an IRA when withdrawing money in case of an emergency.

Phase 2: Normal Distribution

After age 59½, you may take money with out tax-free earnings unless you have not satisfied the 5-year holding period. In this case, you would be subject to income tax and 10% penalty on the earnings only.

Your first Roth IRA contribution starts the 5-year holding period. It is once-in-a-lifetime satisfaction of the holding period rules for all of your Roth IRAs. A subsequent contribution will not start a new holding period.

41

The 5-year holding period for a beneficiary of a Roth IRA includes the time held by the deceased.

Phase 3: Required Minimum Distribution

The best part of a Roth IRA is that there is no RMD after age 70½ for you or your spouse as the beneficiary. The only time a Roth IRA would have a RMD is for a nonspousal beneficiary. You can leave the money in your account for as long as you live or take as much as you need of earnings tax-free (remembering the 5-year rule). The second best part is that you can add more contributions to your Roth IRA (if you have earned income and qualify), as there are no age limits that apply.

Phase 4: Distribution after Death

After you die, your spouse can roll over the money in a Roth IRA in their name and take money out or leave it there as long as they live. There is no RMD for them either. However, if your spouse is under age 59½, it may be advisable to move to a Beneficiary Roth IRA for the benefit of the spouse. In this case, should the spouse need to take money out before age 59½, it would not be subject to the 10% penalty or income tax (as long as the 5-year rule is satisfied).

If the beneficiary is someone other than the spouse, it gets much more complicated. You should seek the advice of a CPA or other tax specialist as these complications have the potential of losing most of the tax benefits. (See the discussion above on IRA for trust.) Nonspouse beneficiaries have three choices:

42

- To take the money in lump sum and pay no income tax or penalty (as long as the deceased held the Roth IRA for more than 5 years);
- Take it out over 5 years and pay no income tax or penalty (as long as the deceased held the Roth IRA for 5 years or more);
- Take lifetime money out based on IRS Minimum Requirement Distribution rules (see Appendix D) and pay no income tax or penalty as he or she takes it out (if the deceased held it for more than 5 years).

The payout is based on the life of the nonspouse beneficiary (this strategy, called Stretch Roth IRA, will be discussed in Chapter 8). If the beneficiary dies prior to depleting the Roth IRA and there is a contingent beneficiary on the account, then the contingent beneficiary will be able to use the remaining value of the account based on the original number of years left based on the nonspouse beneficiary's life expectancy.

Table 7.1: Summarized Comparison of IRA vs. Roth IRA

		IRA	Roth IRA
Phase 1	Accumulation, up to age 59½		
	Contribution	Until age 70½	No age limit
	Distribution	Tax and penalty on all	Tax and penalty on income portion only
Phase 2	Normal Distribution from 59½ to 70½	Taxable	Tax-free earnings if Qualified Roth IRA
phase 3	Required Minimum Distribution, after 70½	Mandatory minimum distribution	None
		Additional contribution not allowed	Contribution allowed, if have earned income
Phase 4	Post Death	Rollover allowed to spouse	Same
		Nonspouse require to take RMD	Same

The contingent beneficiary can always choose to take all money at once and pay no income tax or penalty. If the contingent beneficiary uses the RMD, they can always take more, but cannot take less than the RMD. If they fail to take the RMD, there would be a 50% penalty on the amount that is not taken (see Chapter 8 for more details on Stretch IRA or Stretch Roth IRA).

44

Chapter 8
Stretch IRA and Roth IRA

A Stretch IRA (Continual IRA) is utilizing the required minimum distribution to its fullest. This means the owner has the option of taking money out over the owner's life expectancy (Appendix C, Uniform Distribution Table), which then transfers upon death to the spouse. The spouse continues taking money out, but now over the spouse's life expectancy (same, Appendix C, Uniform Distribution Table), which then transfers upon death to the nonspouse beneficiary. The nonspouse beneficiary continues taking money out, but now over the nonspouse's life expectancy (Appendix D). If the nonspouse beneficiary dies before their life expectancy, then their beneficiary would receive payments over the remaining life expectancy of the nonspouse.

A Stretch Roth IRA (Continual Roth IRA) could be better than a Stretch IRA because the required minimum distribution does not apply until the Roth IRA passes on to the nonspouse beneficiary. This means the owner and spouse are not required to take any distribution; therefore, if the owner or spouse does not need the money and does not take money out of a Roth IRA, there could potentially be more money available to the nonspouse beneficiaries. This is the current law; however, the tax law may change in the future and take this advantage away.

It is one good ways to accumulate money tax-deferred to the next generation (if an IRA) or even tax-free earnings (as a Roth IRA). However, it must be prepared correctly and must follow strict IRS rules.

45

Many people, through marketing and/or advisors and insurance agents, believe that the Stretch IRA is a new or different IRA or, in some cases, even an investment type. I get calls from many clients who have attended some of these seminars and want me to set up a Stretch IRA account for them. As you can see from my explanation, a Stretch IRA is a strategy not an investment type.

Since 2007, a retirement account such as a 401(k), TSA, 403(b) or profit-sharing plan left with the company that you worked for is also eligible for the Stretch IRA. However, it is very easy to miss the steps and the timing of the steps that the company and the beneficiary must follow. When this happens, your beneficiary may end up paying taxes on a lump sum distribution, which, in many cases, is being taxed at the highest bracket and the Stretch IRA is lost forever.

Therefore, I strongly recommend that you rollover your retirement account from your company-sponsored plan into your own IRA. The old saying is, "If you want something done right, do it yourself."

Do not leave anything to chance.

In summary, unlike an IRA there is no RMD for a Roth IRA when you reach 70½ years old. It also passes to your spouse (upon death of the owner) and there is no RMD for the spouse either. A nonspouse beneficiary can stretch the earnings tax-free until the account is depleted.

Chapter 9
Roth 401(k) Plans

Starting in 2006, Roth 401(k) and Roth 403(b) plans were allowed to be offered by employers that provide 401(k) or 403(b) plans to their employees. A Roth 401(k) Plan follows the same tax rules as a Roth IRA, tax-free income after age 59½. The main difference is the amount of contribution allowed into the Roth 401(k). For 2009, if under age 50, the limit is $16,500 and $22,000 if over age 50. If the company offers both 401(k) and Roth 401(k), the maximum contribution applies to both. Therefore, if you are over 50 years old, you could contribute $11,000 to a Roth 401(k) and $11,000 to the 401(k), or contribute in any other combination.

One major difference between a regular 401(k) and a Roth 401(k) is that if the 401(k) plan offers a matching contribution, the match can be on the regular 401(k) but not the Roth 401(k) portion. Even though the IRS allows $16,500 ($22,000 for those over 50 years old), the company may have their own dollar or percentage limits (not to exceed the IRS limits) for the employee's contribution.

Many clients ask whether to do a Roth 401(k) or a regular 401(k). This all depends on an individual's tax situation (such as their current tax bracket and potential tax bracket during retirement), the amount of assets they have and their retirement plan. I do not usually like to make a blanket statement (because everyone has different needs), but if I had to choose one, I would contribute as much into the 401(k) plan as needed in order to receive the maximum

47

employer match (free money!), and then contribute the balance to the Roth 401(k).

There is a RMD for a Roth 401(k) Plan. However, that could be avoided by rolling over the Roth 401(k) into a Roth IRA before the owner's death. Once it is changed to a Roth IRA, the RMD does not apply.

Chapter 10
Thrift Savings Plan

Some companies offer a thrift saving plan. Most of these plans allow after-tax contributions. This means that after you have paid taxes, you can save more for retirement. The money you invest is tax-free when withdrawn (since you have already paid income tax on it when initially earned it), but the earnings are growing tax-deferred. When you retire or change jobs, the money that you invested with after-tax money can be withdrawn without paying tax. The earnings can be rolled over into an IRA and grow tax-deferred until withdrawn. You pay the income tax when the earnings are withdrawn. The rollovers from these funds are subject to required minimum distribution (RMD).

As far as the investments are concerned, your choices are limited to investment options the company offers. Prior to 1998, thrift savings plans were okay because many people used these plans to save more than the 401(k) plan allowed them to save. However, since the 401(k) limits have increased, the thrift savings plan has become obsolete for most people especially after 1998 with the introduction of the Roth IRA. However, many companies still offer these plans and many people still use them.

In my opinion, there is absolutely no reason to put your money in this type of plan if you can save it in a Roth IRA for the reasons described previously. If you are investing in a plan like this where you work, it may be to your benefit to discontinue that plan and start a Roth IRA after discussing it with your advisor.

One planning opportunity you may have is that if you have a thrift saving plan in place, most employers allow you to rollover the earnings into an IRA, which would allow you to continue the tax-deferral on the growth. The remaining after-tax portion would be distributed to you tax-free. Therefore, this money could be used to start or maximize a Roth IRA, which would accumulate tax-free. This can be done even if you are still working for a company and are under 59½ years old.

Some may argue that a thrift savings plan is easy because it is it taken directly out of their paycheck. In fact, all an individual has to do is close this fund account, set up a Roth IRA account and have the same amount of money deducted systematically from a checking account to the investment company.

Chapter 11
Should I Rollover My 401(k) into an IRA?

I know some people leave their retirement plan with the company they worked for after separation because they are misinformed. The following are some of these myths:

Myth #1: "Well I get better pricing and lower fees because the company is paying the fees." That is not true. The company may be paying the fee for the tax and legal issues (administrative costs) of the plan, but they do not pay for the investment part. In fact, in some cases you are paying more because the company does not pay for all the costs of administration and the employee's money subsidizes it. It may be necessary to leave your money with your current company retirement plan if you are still working for the company, but not once you have retired or left the company. However, there are a few cases in which the company would limit you from transferring your retirement amount to an IRA until you reach a certain age, usually age 55. In this case, make sure you complete the rollover as soon as you are able to do so.

Myth #2: "The Company is managing my money." Not true. The company will choose some investment options for the plan, but you must choose your specific investment options.

Myth #3: "I worked for the company all my life, therefore they protect my money." Again, not true. It all depends on what investment options you choose. Some plans have a fixed account or money market account that earns a fixed rate of return and the principal is safe. It is not that the

51

company is protecting your money, but rather that the investments you chose are safe.

Myth #4: "It is just easier to leave it there." This is true, but at what cost? The cost is not allowing your beneficiary the option to control the IRA themselves, but rather the company that set up the 401(K) Plan. It is very easy to transfer your money out, especially if you are working with an advisor. The advisor normally fills out all the paperwork for you.

Section Two

How to Invest your Roth IRA

Chapter 12
The Basics of Investments

When preparing to write about the Roth IRA, I had originally planned to make this a very simple explanation of how and why everyone should have a Roth IRA. Nevertheless, the more I thought about it the more I realized that explaining the Roth IRA is only half the story. After explaining a Roth IRA to clients, typically, the next question is, "how do I get one?" That is when I knew I had to educate clients that the Roth IRA is a retirement plan not an investment plan. How you make money depends on the type of investments you choose. I will show you how to look for an advisor to help you set one up or do it yourself in section two. In my next edition of this book I will talk more about specific investment options.

How and where do you invest your money?

The following is a partial list of categories in which you can invest the IRA or Roth IRA money:

- Money market
- Certificate of deposit (CD)
- Mutual funds
- Stocks
- Bonds
- Fixed annuities
- Variable annuities
- Indexed (or equity) fixed annuity
- REIT
- Oil and gas
- Real estate
- Leasing

54

Which one you choose depends on the time and the purposes for saving the money, as well as the type of investor you are.

Which one of these choices is best for you? It depends on you.

The following is a partial list of categories and items in which you cannot invest and things you are not allowed to do with the IRA or Roth IRA money:

- Borrowing money from it
- Selling property to it
- Using it as securities for a loan
- Buying property for personal use
- Purchase of collectibles such as:
  - Artworks
  - Rugs
  - Antiques
  - Metals
  - Gems
  - Stamps
  - Coins

  One exception within IRA or Roth IRA is that you can invest in one, one-half, one-quarter, or one-tenth ounce U.S. gold coins, or one-ounce silver coins minted by the Treasury department. It is possible with an IRA or Roth IRA to invest in certain platinum coins and certain gold, silver, palladium, and platinum bullion. You must find a custodian such as a bank or trust company to

hold these assets and act as the trustee.
- Alcoholic beverages

However before publishing the next edition of this book, I would like to discuss some of the myths about investments and in addition, give some information on how to use information you come across.

One of the biggest concerns I have with some people writing books, or having a talk show or a newspaper column is that they become very biased in their opinions. They stress that their ideas are right for everyone and meanwhile everything else is wrong. I will give a few examples of these biased opinions so you will know what I am talking about. Then, the next time you read one of these articles or listen to the discussion, you can make a more informed decision. Here are some examples of biased opinions:

- No-load fund is the only way to invest in mutual funds.
- Only invest in low-fee mutual funds.
- You should invest in index funds only.
- Annuities are bad.
- Managed accounts are the only way to invest.
- Fee-based is the only way to go.
- "I heard it on the radio," or "I read it in a book, so it must be impartial or correct."
- In a seminar, the speaker states that you should only do index annuities, managed accounts, or says that CDs are not good, or you will lose your money in variable annuities.

56

When you hear any of the statements above, you should run as fast as you can! They are not addressing your particular circumstances; they are simply recommending what is easiest for them or what makes the most money for them. They are using their own biases for everyone else. They believe that their one shoe fits everyone!

Before you invest in your Roth IRA or any other investment, you need to know and understand some components of any investment.

They are:

- Time horizon
- Risk of inflation
- Tax consequences
- Knowledge and or experience with investments
- Investment objectives
- Risk tolerance

I believe that anyone investing without proper understanding of these elements is doing himself or herself an injustice. I will discuss some of these items next.

57

Investment Horizon (Time Line)

Investment horizon is defined as the amount of time you need to keep the money invested before it is used for the purpose intended.

- **Short-term** means you need to use the money in less than 3 years. It could be savings for emergency money, for a down payment on a car, to purchase an appliance, or to go on vacation.

- **Mid-term** means you need to use the money in approximately the next 3 to 10 years. It can be saved to buy a new car, as a down payment on a house, a special vacation such as an anniversary, going overseas, a once-in-a-lifetime vacation, a major appliance such as a complete home entertainment center, or saving for college.

- **Long-term** means you can usually wait 10 years or longer to use the money. This is typically for a large down payment on a house or vacation home, saving for college or, most importantly, for retirement. Now, once you retire, this does not mean that all your money needs to move to short-term. Only the portion that you need for the next 3 years and then the portion that you need for the next 3 to 10 years need to be invested accordingly. One of the biggest mistakes I see is when a retiree takes all of their money and invests it as if they need it within 3 years. In reality, a person who retires at age 65 has a life expectancy of 88. That is over 20 years of continued investing for that money.

58

Risk

Any investment has a risk. I can already hear someone saying that is not true! The CD has no risk. There are two types of risks to discuss. The first is not earning enough interest to offset inflation (see below) and to pay income taxes (such as investing in CDs and bonds). The second risk is losing the principal, as with stocks, even though they have a greater potential to earn enough interest to offset inflation and taxes. So when discussing risk, one must consider the risk of not earning enough as well as the risk of losing principal.

What is inflation? Simply put, the cost of what you buy a year from now will typically be more than its cost today. In the last few years, average inflation has been around 3% (according to Bureau of labor Statistics the average inflation from 1986 to 2008 was 2.99% per year). That means, on average, the price of everything will be 3% more next year. For example, a pair of shoes that cost $100 today would be $103 next year, $106.90 in 2 years, $134.39 in 10 years, and double in about 23 years (see Table 12.1, which shows the effect of inflation on your money depending on different inflation rates). If the average inflation rate is 3%, that does not mean everything is going up by 3%. Some items may go up more than 3% such as health and medical costs. The cost of some items, such as computers and other electronics, may actually go down. The average ends up being around 3%. Inflation may affect two people entirely differently, depending on what you buy. What does this mean to you as an investor? If inflation were 3%, then the first 3% you make on your investment would only offset inflation. So if your investment in a money market account, for example, only makes 3% a year on average over the

59

next 10 to 20 years it may seem that you have more money, however, because the average costs will go up, you would not be able to buy what you can today without an increase in your earning power.

What Is Inflation?

1940
34 cents

2008
$4.28

60

Table 12.1: Inflation schedule – How Much You Need in the Future Based on Various Inflation Rates

Year		3.00%	3.50%	4.00%
1	100.00	103.00	103.50	104.00
2	0.00	106.09	107.12	108.16
3	0.00	109.27	110.87	112.49
4	0.00	112.55	114.75	116.99
5	0.00	115.93	118.77	121.67
6	0.00	119.41	122.93	126.53
7	0.00	122.99	127.23	131.59
8	0.00	126.68	131.68	136.86
9	0.00	130.48	136.29	142.33
10	0.00	134.39	141.06	148.02
11	0.00	138.42	146.00	153.95
12	0.00	142.58	151.11	160.10
13	0.00	151.26	161.87	173.17
14	0.00	155.80	167.53	180.09
15	0.00	160.47	173.40	187.30
16	0.00	165.28	179.47	194.79
17	0.00	170.24	185.75	202.58
18	0.00	175.35	192.25	210.68
19	0.00	180.61	198.98	219.11
20	0.00	186.03	205.94	227.88
21	0.00	191.61	213.15	236.99
22	0.00	197.36	220.61	246.47
23	0.00	203.28	228.33	256.33
24	0.00	209.38	236.32	266.58
25	0.00	215.66	244.60	277.25
26	0.00	222.13	253.16	288.34
27	0.00	228.79	262.02	299.87
28	0.00	235.66	271.19	311.87
29	0.00	242.73	280.68	324.34
30	0.00	250.01	290.50	337.31

Taxes

Income taxes are one of the three highest expenses for most families, next to mortgage (or rent) and insurance (health, life, disability, and long-term care). Therefore, how and when you pay taxes matters. Some investments are tax-free, some tax-deferred and some are taxable as you go.

Obviously, Roth IRA earnings are tax-free, and that is why I am writing this book.

The next group is tax-deferred investments, such as an IRA, 401(k) or any other type of retirement plan on which you did not pay tax at the time of investment or deferred paying tax on the earrings until withdrawn.

The last group is taxable investments. They are taxable as they pay interest, dividends, or capital gains, even if you do not use or reinvest the earnings. These would be any investments other than retirement accounts.

For 2008, the tax rate for federal income tax is from 10% to 33%. State income taxes vary by state. A few states have no income tax. When investing, you must take into account the amount of all taxes you are paying.

In the next few chapters, I will touch on a few other topics before discussing the actual investing, as some of these topics will apply to all or some of the investment options discussed in Section Four. I will also cover some of the myths that I have mentioned or that you may be hearing.

Chapter 13
Who Should Handle Your Investments?

Do It Yourself

These investors like to be in charge of their own investing. They study the investment they purchase in depth. They are typically the investors who have investment 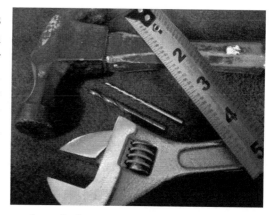 knowledge. They do their own research and are comfortable with their knowledge of various investments. Many have made good overall investment decisions and have accumulated substantial wealth because of their knowledge. However, there are others doing their own investing whom, unfortunately, bypasses all the hard work of research. They choose their investments from the hottest fund of last year or in the last 3 years based on rumor, what their friends tell them, what they see in money magazines, or on unreliable sources. In many cases, as soon as they buy the funds, most of them go cold or lose money. These individuals may have a tendency to blame the market for being risky, sell the investment then, and settle for a money market rate. Even worse, some actually stop investing with the idea that investing is not making them any money and they would rather enjoy their money now instead of lose it in the market. I have heard many times from some of these

63

investors, "I am messing around with some stocks." How can you mess around with your hard-earned money?

If you do choose to do it yourself, then do it right! There are no shortcuts. You must research the product you are investing in. Invest in what you know.

If you are not willing to learn and research, it is best if you stay away from investing in the stock market and use a professional.

Hire a Professional

Investors who are not comfortable with their level of investment knowledge or do not have the time to do their own investing should hire a financial professional. Financial professionals come in many shapes. We will discuss different kinds of advisors first and then how they are paid. First, what types of financial professional are out there?

Fee-Based Advisors

A fee-based advisor normally charges an hourly fee or a flat rate based on the time it takes for them to do a financial plan. Some Fee-based advisors have Certified Financial Planner™ (CFP®) designation. Typically, they provide an asset allocation or other goals for you. Many times they do not provide specific investment options or recommend what to buy. They will tell you, for instance, that you should invest 30% in large companies or 15% in small companies. Alternatively, they determine how much you need to save (say $500 a month) earning at 8% for the next

10 or 20 years to achieve your retirement goals or have adequate money to take your dream vacation.

Some advisors may refer you to a broker who can implement the asset allocation with actual investments. Some of them work in offices with other advisors who provide the actual investments. Other advisors will implement the investments themselves and are paid a commission or fee (which will be discussed next). Make sure you know the arrangement.

An Investment Advisor Representative will manage your money by charging you a fee that represents a percentage of your account value.

Some people believe that, Fee-based advisors tend to be unbiased since they receive a fee and there is no additional income derived from the sale of the investment products. Even though that may be the case, because they do not sell products, they may still be biased toward some products based on there own investment preferences even though some of these investments may not be appropriate for certain clients.

Some advisors charge a small fee for financial planning with the hope of investing your money later. There is nothing wrong with this as long as you are aware of the arrangement. I have no problem with advisors making a living, but they need to be honest with you. You trust them with your money and they must be honest with you.

Commission-Based Brokers

Commission-based Brokers are paid by selling and servicing a product. Some charge the commission against the investment, while others net the commissions against the earnings. I do hear a common theme that, "The banks do not charge me any fees on my CD or money market." Well, how do you think they pay for their building and employees? Of course, they are netting their fees into the rates they offer. For example, the bank makes loans to consumers at 7%, but only pays you 4% on your CD. What happens to the difference? You can consider the difference of 3% as the commission or fee. What you should know is that if the financial professional is not charging you a fee, then he or she is getting paid a commission. Therefore, if a professional tells you he is not charging you anything, you must wonder how he makes money. It is certainly okay for you to ask a professional you work with how they are paid. They should be very comfortable in discussing it. It is important that you work with a professional who is right for you!

Some professionals may provide products on which they receive commissions, while offering managed accounts for others.

66

Chapter 14
Who Provides Investment Advice?

The U.S. Securities and Exchange Commission (SEC) is the government agency that monitors investment professionals and the investment product.

The Financial Industry Regulatory Authority (FINRA) requires its members (broker/dealers) to follow the SEC rules.

Registered Investment Advisor

Registered Investment Advisor is set up to monitor the advisors who provide fee-based services to clients in order to ensure that they follow all the SEC rules.

Broker/Dealer

A broker/dealer is set up to monitor the brokers who sell and service the clients in order to ensure that they follow all the SEC and FINRA rules. Broker/dealers may provide such services to their brokers who are registered representative of the firm.

Typically, the broker/dealer offers a variety of investment options because they support many advisors with different needs. The followings are some of the broker/advisors:

Wirehouses

These large Wall Street firms provide sales and service of various investments and own their own broker/dealer. They

67

are usually located in the large office buildings of downtown areas. Contrary to popular belief, even though they are large firms, many of them may not provide the variety of investment options. Some examples are Morgan Stanley, Merrill Lynch and CitiGroup.

Brokers are employees of the brokerage firm and they receive a percentage of the commissions that the firm earns from the sale of products.

Bank Branches

These professionals are located in banks, savings and loan associations, or credit unions. They are usually set up as legal entities separate from the banks. Some of the larger banks own their own broker/dealers while some smaller banks use independent broker/dealers. The banks may own them, but they operate independently. They do, however, market to the bank customers and may receive referrals from the bank staff. They will have notices posted in their offices and marketing literature stating that their investments are not FDIC insured so that customers do not think they are investing in bank products that are FDIC insured. Some examples are Bank of America and Community America Credit Union.

Some Brokers are employees of the bank and they receive a percentage of the commissions that the bank earns from the sale of products.

Independent Agents

These agents work for themselves and provide their own office and staff. These professionals normally choose the

68

investments that are appropriate for their investors. One professional in this group may only do managed accounts, while another may sell only oil and gas. Yet another may offer a little of everything that the broker/dealer offers. These advisors use broker/dealers such as Berthel Fisher & Company Financial Services, Inc., LPL Financial, and Next Financial.

Independent Agents receive commissions from the sale of products or they charge fees for managed accounts if they are Investment Advisor Representatives.

Insurance Agents

In the past, insurance agents only sold insurance. In recent years, they have added investments as an additional product. Most insurance agents work for an insurance company and are only allowed to sell the investments that their insurance company provides. However, because of the competitiveness of the market, some of these insurance agents are also able to sell products of another company. These options are still limited, but it is better than having no choice except their own products. Not all insurance agents deal with investments because it does require additional licensing to sell securities other than fixed insurance products. Some of the larger insurance companies own their own broker/dealer such as State Farm Insurance, Farmers Insurance, and Northwestern Life Insurance, while some smaller insurance companies use an independent broker/dealer.

Agents are employees or statuary employees of the insurance companies and receive a percentage of commissions that the company earns from the sale of product.

Free Advice

You know what you get for free. This is the free advice you may receive from friends, neighbors, radio talk shows, or from investment company advertisements about their past performance (which is not a guarantee for the future performance). The problem is that, although this free advice may be good advice, it may not be appropriate for your situation. It may work well for the one giving the advice, but not necessarily for you.

Who should handle it?

- Yourself
- A Professional
- Fee-Based Advisors
- Commission-Based Brokers
- Wirehouses
- Bank Branches
- Independent Agents
- Insurance Agents

70

Section Three

Tax Saving Strategies

Chapter 15
Finding Tax Savings

There are many ways to save taxes. Certain items save taxes currently, while others delay paying taxes, and yet others save taxes only on the earnings. The following is a partial listing of some of these tax-saving strategies. Even though they apply to all taxpayers, some of these tax savings may be subject to phase-out rules based on income, age, or certain other conditions. In the following chapters, you will see about 125 different tax credits and deductions that can save you money.

72

Chapter 16
Tax Credits

A tax credit is the best form of a tax-savings program. Tax credits will reduce your income taxes dollar for dollar. For example, a $100 tax credit saves $100 in income tax. Some credits are refundable, meaning the tax credit first reduces your income tax, and then, if the credit is in excess of your tax liability, it will be refunded. The second type is nonrefundable, which means they only reduce the tax to zero and you would not receive any refund for the remainder. Some of the nonrefundable credits would carry over to future years, while others would be lost. Here is a partial list of the personal tax credits:

Refundable
- Earned income credit
- Health coverage credit
- Federal tax on fuels
- Farm use/off-highway business use

Partially Refundable
- Additional child credit

Nonrefundable
- Child and dependent care credit
- Education credit (Hope scholarship, Lifetime learning)
- Elderly or disabled credit
- Hybrid vehicle credit
- Retirement saver's credit

Generally nonrefundable

73

- Child credit

Nonrefundable/carry forward (CF) 3 years
- Mortgage Interest credit

Nonrefundable/CF 5 years
- Adoption expense credit

Nonrefundable/carry back 1 year, CF 10 years
- Foreign tax credit

Partially refundable/CF indefinitely
- Minimum tax credit
- Residential energy credit

For business owners there are general business tax credits:
- Alcohol fuels credit
- Biodiesel and renewable diesel fuel credit
- Community development credit
- Disabled access
- Distilled spirits credit
- Employer-paid FICA on tips
- Employer-provided child care credit
- Empowerment zone and renewal
- Community employment credit
- Energy credits
- Enhanced oil recovery credit
- Indian employment credit
- Investment credit
- Energy credit
- Qualifying advanced coal project
- Qualifying gasification project
- Rehabilitation credit

- Low-income housing credit
- Low-sulfur diesel fuel production credit
- Marginal oil and gas credit
- Mine rescue team training credit
- New markets credit
- Nonconventional source fuel credit
- Nuclear power facility
- Orphan drug credit
- Pension plan start-up costs credit (small employers)
- Railroad track maintenance credit
- Refined coal and Indian coal production credit
- Renewable electricity credit
- Research credit
- Work opportunity credit

Chapter 17
Tax Deductions

Tax deductions reduce your taxable income. Any tax benefits are based on your tax bracket. Therefore, if your tax bracket for federal tax were 15%, 25%, or 33%, then you would save 15%, 25%, or 33% tax on the amount of your deductions. You could save tax at your highest tax bracket by using tax deductions.

For example, the tax brackets (income less all your deductions) for a single person for the 2007 tax year were as follows:

- From $1 to $7,825, the tax rate is 10%
- From $7,825 to $31,850, the tax rate is 15%
- From $31,850 to $77,100, the tax rate is 25%
- From $77,100 to $160,850, the tax rate is 28%
- From $160,850 to $349,700, the tax rate is 33%
- Any amount above $349,700 is taxed at 35%

So for example, if you had income of $35,000 and tax deductions of $5,000, you would save income tax based on two brackets. You would save 25% in income taxes on the first $3,150 in deductions, and you would save 15% in income taxes on the remaining $1,850 in deductions. This occurs because your income is close to the threshold amount. The calculations are as follows:

$35,000 − $31,850 = $3,150
$5,000 − $3,150 = $1,850
$3,150 x 25% = $787.50
$1,850 x 15% = $277.50

76

The total tax savings is $1,065).

There are two types of deductions; the first type reduces your income directly (also called "above the line"), and the second type is bunched together (itemized deductions). If deductions are over a certain amount, depending on your filing status (single, married filing as joint, married filing separately, or head of household), they will reduce your taxable income.

The following is a partial listing of deductions that directly reduce your income (above the line):

- Alimony paid
- Education expenses
- Health insurance savings accounts
- Moving expenses
- Self-employed health insurance
- Student loan interest

The next lists of deductions are added together and are treated as itemized deductions (Schedule A). Your income is reduced by the higher of the standard deduction (for 2007, it was $5,350 for a single, $10,700 for married people or $7,850 for head of household) or your itemized deductions.

Itemized deductions are the total of all the following items:

- Medical deductions can be taken if, in aggregate, your expenses are more than 7.5% of your adjusted gross income. This is list of just some of the qualified medical expenses:
  o Health insurance premium

77

- o Long-term care insurance premium (with limits)
- o Prescription medicine
- o Eyeglasses/eye surgery
- o Continuing-care facilities
- o Travel to doctor's office/hospital

- State taxes paid
- Real estate taxes paid for personal residence
- Real estate taxes paid for land or investment property
- Personal property tax
- Foreign taxes
- Mortgage interest for a personal residence
- Mortgage interest on investment property
- Interest on home equity loan
- Mortgage points on principal residence
- Mortgage points on refinancing
- Seller-paid mortgage points
- Mortgage interest paid on second home
- Construction loan interest
- Interest paid on timeshare
- Interest paid on boats
- Interest paid on mobile and house trailers
- Reverse mortgage interest
- Mortgage insurance premium

- Contributions paid to charities in the form of a check or with receipts
- Cash donations (substantiation is required)
- Noncash donations (substantiation is required)

- Casualty losses (special rules apply):

78

- Car accident
- Earthquakes
- Fire
- Floods
- Hurricanes
- Storm
- Thefts
- Tornados
- Vandalism
- Some others

- Estate taxes paid in respect of a decedent
- Gambling losses (to the extent of gambling winnings)
- Special job-related expenses of handicapped (readers and aides)
- Unrecovered cost of annuities (on decedent's last tax return)

The following deductions apply if, in aggregate, they are more than 2% of your adjusted gross income:
- Appraisal fees for charitable donations
- Appraisal cost (casualty losses)
- Clerical help for maintaining investments
- Fees to collect interest or dividends
- Hobby expenses (up to the amount of hobby income)
- Investment expenses (research)
- Investment expenses (managed fees)
- Fee paid for custodial IRA
- Job hunting
- Job-related education (special rules apply)
- Legal fees to collect taxable income

- Loss on deposits in insolvent or bankrupt financial institutions
- Losses on a Roth IRA that has been distributed fully
- Medical examinations required by employer
- Union and professional dues
- Safe deposit box
- Tax-preparation fees
- Trust administration fees
- Undeveloped land management fees
- Work clothes and uniforms that are required by employer and not suitable to use for normal wear

Some people buy a bigger house to save money on their income taxes. It is true that you save income tax on the interest, but your savings is only based on your tax bracket. For example, if you pay $10,000 in mortgage interest and you are in the 25% tax bracket, you will save $2,500 in taxes; but you had to pay the mortgage company or bank $10,000 to save $2,500. Therefore, it still costs you $7,500. Obviously, not many people can buy a house for cash, but do not get a bigger mortgage because it is tax deductible. The worst thing someone can do is spend more money on items like mortgage interest because it is deductible. This is also true for any other deduction; so, do not spend money just to get the tax deductions. Only spend money on what you need, and if you get a tax benefit, that is great!

Chapter 18
Tax Deferred

These deductions only delay the payment of taxes. They reduce your income currently, but when taken out, you pay tax based on your tax bracket at that time. There are times when you may never pay tax on them (for example, if when taken out, your taxable income is low or you have other deductions that cause you to pay no tax). We discussed these in detail in the prior chapters. They are as follows:

- IRA
- 401(k) plan
- SEP/IRA
- Simple IRA
- 403(b) or TSA
- 457 plans
- Money purchase plan
- Profit-sharing plan

The second type does not reduce your current income but defers paying taxes on the earnings until it is withdrawn. These were discussed in detail in the prior chapters. They are as follows:

- Fixed annuity
- Fixed index annuity
- Variable annuity

81

Chapter 19
Tax Free

A tax-free investment is one for which you do not get a tax deduction for the investment, but the earnings are tax-free.

We discussed some of these tax-free incomes previously. They are as follows:

- Qualified Roth IRA (discussed in detail as the main subject of this book)
- Qualified Roth IRA 401(k) Plan
- Municipal bonds purchased from resident's state (exempt from federal and state taxes)
- Municipal bonds purchased from out of state (exempt from federal tax)
- Government bonds (exempt from state tax, but subject to federal tax)

If you usually receive a refund of $300 or more a year, you should change your W-4 and increase your exemptions by one or more. This will give you more money in each paycheck. Then, set up a Roth IRA savings plan that allows you to save every month. When filing your tax return, if you owe money, then you can take the money from the savings and pay the tax, but keep the interest. Alternatively, if you were using this refund for a specific plan, do so but leave the interest. This allows you to keep the earnings from the investment versus the IRS having it. You can take this one step further and plan to use your refund plus up to $1,000 more (you can owe the IRS up to $1,000 a year and pay it by April 15 when your income tax is due, and pay no interest or penalty). Many investment companies allow you to invest as little as $25 per month. See Appendix A to see how much your money can grow just by investing $50 per month.

APPENDIX A

Hypothetical illustration when investing $50 a month ($600 per year starting at age 20) at different rates of return

Age	AMOUNT Invested	Earning 4.00%	Earning 6.00%	Earning 8.00%	Earning 9.00%	Earning 10.00%	Earning 12.00%
20	$600	$624	$636	$648	$654	$660	$672
21	600	1,273	1,310	1,348	1,367	1,386	1,425
22	600	1,948	2,025	2,104	2,144	2,185	2,268
23	600	2,650	2,782	2,920	2,991	3,063	3,212
24	600	3,380	3,585	3,802	3,914	4,029	4,269
25	600	4,139	4,436	4,754	4,920	5,092	5,453
26	600	4,929	5,338	5,782	6,017	6,262	6,780
27	600	5,750	6,295	6,893	7,213	7,548	8,265
28	600	6,604	7,308	8,092	8,516	8,962	9,929
29	600	7,492	8,383	9,387	9,936	10,519	11,793
30	600	8,415	9,522	10,786	11,484	12,231	13,880
31	600	9,376	10,729	12,297	13,172	14,114	16,217
32	600	11,414	13,366	15,691	17,017	18,463	21,768
33	600	12,495	14,804	17,595	19,202	20,970	25,052
34	600	13,619	16,328	19,650	21,584	23,727	28,730
35	600	14,787	17,943	21,870	24,181	26,760	32,850
36	600	16,003	19,656	24,268	27,011	30,095	37,464
37	600	17,267	21,471	26,857	30,096	33,765	42,631
38	600	18,582	23,396	29,654	33,459	37,801	48,419
39	600	19,949	25,435	32,674	37,124	42,242	54,902
40	600	21,371	27,597	35,936	41,119	47,126	62,162
41	600	22,850	29,889	39,459	45,474	52,498	70,293
42	600	24,388	32,319	43,264	50,221	58,408	79,400
43	600	25,987	34,894	47,373	55,394	64,909	89,600
44	600	27,651	37,623	51,810	61,034	72,060	101,024
45	600	29,381	40,517	56,603	67,181	79,926	113,819
46	600	31,180	43,584	61,780	73,881	88,579	128,150
47	600	33,051	46,835	67,370	81,185	98,096	144,200
48	600	34,997	50,281	73,408	89,145	108,566	162,176
49	600	37,021	53,934	79,928	97,822	120,083	182,309
50	600	39,126	57,806	86,970	107,280	132,751	204,858
51	600	41,315	61,910	94,576	117,589	146,686	230,113

83

Age	AMOUNT Invested	Earning 4.00%	Earning 6.00%	Earning 8.00%	Earning 9.00%	Earning 10.00%	Earning 12.00%
52	600	43,591	66,261	102,790	128,826	162,015	258,398
53	600	45,959	70,873	111,661	141,075	178,876	290,078
54	600	48,421	75,761	121,242	154,426	197,424	325,559
55	600	50,982	80,943	131,590	168,978	217,826	365,298
56	600	53,645	86,435	142,765	184,840	240,269	409,806
57	600	56,415	92,257	154,834	202,129	264,956	459,655
58	600	59,296	98,429	167,869	220,975	292,111	515,485
59	600	62,292	104,970	181,946	241,517	321,982	578,016
60	600	65,407	111,905	197,150	263,907	354,840	648,050
61	600	68,648	119,255	213,570	288,313	390,984	726,488
62	600	72,018	127,046	231,303	314,915	430,743	814,338
63	600	75,522	135,305	250,456	343,912	474,477	912,731
64	600	79,167	144,059	271,140	375,518	522,585	1,022,930
65	600	82,958	153,339	293,479	409,968	575,503	1,146,354
Total	28,200						

The interest rates of 4% to 12% are for illustrative purposes only. This is not a guarantee of future interest rates or financial return. This illustration assumes deposits made at the beginning of each year. This illustration does not account for reduction for inflation and taxes.

84

APPENDIX B

Hypothetical illustration when investing $1,600 or $2,000 per year for 10 years in an IRA or ROTH IRA at different rates of return

	IRA before tax investment				Roth IRA after tax investment		
Age	AMOUNT SAVED	Earning 4.00%	Earning 8.00%	Age	AMOUNT SAVED	Earning 4.00%	Earning 8.00%
20	$2,000	$2,080	$2,160	20	$1,600	$1,664	$1,728
21	2,000	4,243	4,493	21	1,600	3,395	3,594
22	2,000	6,493	7,012	22	1,600	5,194	5,610
23	2,000	8,833	9,733	23	1,600	7,066	7,787
24	2,000	11,266	12,672	24	1,600	9,013	10,137
25	2,000	13,797	15,846	25	1,600	11,037	12,676
26	2,000	16,428	19,273	26	1,600	13,143	15,419
27	2,000	19,166	22,975	27	1,600	15,332	18,380
28	2,000	22,012	26,973	28	1,600	17,610	21,578
29	2,000	24,973	31,291	29	1,600	19,978	25,033
30	0	25,972	33,794	30	0	20,777	27,035
31	0	27,010	36,498	31	0	21,608	29,198
32	0	29,215	42,571	32	0	23,372	34,057
33	0	30,383	45,977	33	0	24,306	36,781
34	0	31,598	49,655	34	0	25,279	39,724
35	0	32,862	53,627	35	0	26,290	42,902
36	0	34,177	57,917	36	0	27,341	46,334
37	0	35,544	62,551	37	0	28,435	50,041
38	0	36,966	67,555	38	0	29,573	54,044
39	0	38,444	72,959	39	0	30,755	58,367
40	0	39,982	78,796	40	0	31,986	63,037
41	0	41,581	85,100	41	0	33,265	68,080
42	0	43,245	91,908	42	0	34,596	73,526

	IRA before tax investment				Roth IRA after tax investment		
Age	AMOUNT SAVED	Earning 4.00%	Earning 8.00%	Age	AMOUNT SAVED	Earning 4.00%	Earning 8.00%
43	0	44,974	99,260	43	0	35,980	79,408
44	0	46,773	107,201	44	0	37,419	85,761
45	0	48,644	115,777	45	0	38,915	92,622
46	0	50,590	125,039	46	0	40,472	100,031
47	0	52,614	135,042	47	0	42,091	108,034
48	0	54,718	145,846	48	0	43,775	116,677
49	0	56,907	157,514	49	0	45,526	126,011
50	0	59,183	170,115	50	0	47,347	136,092
51	0	61,551	183,724	51	0	49,240	146,979
52	0	64,013	198,422	52	0	51,210	158,737
53	0	66,573	214,295	53	0	53,259	171,436
54	0	69,236	231,439	54	0	55,389	185,151
55	0	72,006	249,954	55	0	57,604	199,963
56	0	74,886	269,951	56	0	59,909	215,960
57	0	77,881	291,547	57	0	62,305	233,237
58	0	80,996	314,870	58	0	64,797	251,896
59	0	84,236	340,060	59	0	67,389	272,048
60	0	87,606	367,265	60	0	70,085	293,812
61	0	91,110	396,646	61	0	72,888	317,317
62	0	94,754	428,378	62	0	75,803	342,702
63	0	98,545	462,648	63	0	78,836	370,118
64	0	102,486	499,660	64	0	81,989	399,728
65	0	106,586	539,632	65	0	85,269	431,706
66	0	110,849	582,803	66	0	88,679	466,242
Tax	0	(22,170)	(116,561)	Tax	0	0	0
Net Value after tax	20,000	88,679	466,242	Net Value after tax	16,000	88,679	466,242

86

The interest rates of 4% and 8% are for illustrative purposes only. This is not a guarantee of future interest rates or financial return. This illustration assumes deposits made at the beginning of each year. This illustration does not account for reduction for inflation and taxes.

Appendix C
Uniform Distribution Table 2002 (Life Expectancy)

This table is the new life expectancy table to be used by all IRA owners to calculate lifetime distributions (unless your beneficiary is your spouse who is more than 10 years younger than you are). In that case, you would not use this table, you would use the actual joint life expectancy of you and your spouse based on the regular joint life expectancy table. The Uniform Distribution Table is never used by IRA beneficiaries to compute required distributions on their inherited IRAs.

Uniform Distribution Table

Age of IRA Owners (in years)	Life Expectancy	Age of IRA Owners (in years)	Life Expectancy
70	27.4	93	9.6
71	26.5	94	9.1
72	25.6	95	8.6
73	24.7	96	8.1
74	23.8	97	7.6
75	22.9	98	7.1
76	22.0	99	6.7
77	21.2	100	6.3
78	20.3	101	5.9
79	19.5	102	5.5
80	18.7	103	5.2
81	17.9	104	4.9
82	17.1	105	4.5
83	16.3	106	4.2
84	15.5	107	3.9
85	14.8	108	3.7
86	14.1	109	3.4
87	13.4	110	3.1
88	12.7	111	2.9
89	12.0	112	2.6
90	11.4	113	2.4
91	10.8	114	2.1
92	10.2	115 and older	1.9

88

Appendix D

Single Life Expectancy for Use by Beneficiaries

Age of IRA or Roth IRA Beneficiary (in years)	Life Expectancy	Age of IRA or Roth IRA Beneficiary (in years)	Life Expectancy
0	82.4	56	28.7
1	81.6	57	27.9
2	80.6	58	27.0
3	79.7	59	26.1
4	78.7	60	25.2
5	77.7	61	24.4
6	76.7	62	23.5
7	75.8	63	22.7
8	74.8	64	21.8
9	73.8	65	21.0
10	72.8	66	20.2
11	71.8	67	19.4
12	70.8	68	18.6
13	69.9	69	17.8
14	68.9	70	17.0
15	67.9	71	16.3
16	66.9	72	15.5
17	66.0	73	14.8
18	65.0	74	14.1
19	64.0	75	13.4
20	63.0	76	12.7
21	62.1	77	12.1
22	61.1	78	11.4
23	60.1	79	10.8
24	59.1	80	10.2
25	58.2	81	9.7
26	57.2	82	9.1
27	56.2	83	8.6

89

Age of IRA or Roth IRA Beneficiary (in years)	Life Expectancy	Age of IRA or Roth IRA Beneficiary (in years)	Life Expectancy
28	55.3	84	8.1
29	54.3	85	7.6
30	53.3	86	7.1
31	52.4	87	6.7
32	51.4	88	6.3
33	50.4	89	5.9
34	49.4	90	5.5
35	48.5	91	5.2
36	47.5	92	4.9
37	46.5	93	4.6
38	45.6	94	4.3
39	44.6	95	4.1
40	43.6	96	3.8
41	42.7	97	3.6
42	41.7	98	3.4
43	40.7	99	3.1
44	39.8	100	2.9
45	38.8	101	2.7
46	37.9	102	2.5
47	37.0	103	2.3
48	36.0	104	2.1
49	35.1	105	1.9
50	34.2	106	1.7
51	33.3	107	1.5
52	32.3	108	1.4
53	31.4	109	1.2
54	30.5	110	1.1
55	29.6	111 and over	1.0

90

GLOSSARY

401(k) Plan — Company plan set up for employees to contribute to a retirement account before income taxes are paid on the contributions.

403(b) Plan — See TSA Plan.

457 Plans — Similar to a 401(k) plan, but for government and state agencies.

adjusted gross income (AGI) — Total of all income less certain deductions. AGI is used to phase out certain deductions or limits the contribution to an IRA or Roth IRA.

certificate of deposit (CD) — Investing with banks or savings and loan associations that pay a predetermined rate of interest on your money that is held for a specific amount of time.

defined pension plan — When an employer promises to pay the employee a certain amount of money when they retire (what is known as a company pension). Therefore, the company must determine how much to contribute to the plan in order to have enough money to pay employees after they retire.

depreciation — Writing off the cost of a building or equipment over a period allowed by the Internal Revenue Service.

Financial Industry Regulatory Authority (FINRA) — A self-regulatory organization that monitors its members (broker/dealers) to enforce the SEC rules.

individual retirement account — See IRA

inflation — When costs increase every year.

IRA — A retirement account to which contributions can be made before income taxes are paid on that income.

Internal Revenue Service (IRS) — The U.S. government agency that is responsible for collecting taxes and enforcing tax law.

pension plan — Similar to a profit-sharing plan, but the employer is required to contribute each year a certain percentage to each employee's retirement account that was agreed upon when plan was set up.

primary beneficiary — The first person(s) who would receive the balance of any account after the death of the owner of an IRA, Roth IRA, any company retirement accounts, and annuities.

profit-sharing plan — Company plan that contributes to a retirement account for eligible employees and/or owners. An employer can adjust the amount of the contribution each year ranging from zero to 25% of an employee's eligible wages.

qualified Roth IRA — A Roth IRA that has been invested for more than five years and is owned by someone who is more than 59½ years old.

92

required minimum distribution (RMD) — After age 70½, you must take a distribution from all of your IRAs, or any company retirement plan such as 401(k) plans. It is common for people to call it RMD.

Roth IRA conversion — When a regular IRA is converted to a Roth IRA. It becomes taxable at the time of conversion.

Roth IRA — Contributing after-tax money for retirement.

Securities and Exchange Commission (SEC) — Government agency that regulates the investment companies, investment rules, and investment products.

Simplified employee pension/Individual retirement account (SEP/IRA) — Like an IRA, but set up by employers to contribute before tax money to the employee's or owner's retirement plan.

SIMPLE IRA — Setup by a company for employees or by self-employed individuals to contribute income to a retirement account before income taxes are paid on it.

Solo 401(k) Plan — Similar to a 401(k) plan, but set up for small companies to allow contributions for owners that do not have employees.

Stretch IRA and Roth IRA — When taking distributions from an IRA or Roth IRA over the owner's and then the beneficiary's life expectancy.

thrift savings plan — Contribution to a company retirement plan with after-tax money.

TSA plan — Employee's contribution to a retirement account before income taxes are paid on it, similar to a 401(k), but set up by nonprofit entities and some government agencies.

Bibliography

For those who want to learn more about investing or learn more about specific topics, I recommend the following:

For stocks and equity investing:
How Buffett Does It, James Pardoe

Simple Wealth, Inevitable Wealth, Nick Murray

Stocks for the Long Run, 4th edition, Jeremy Siegel

For bond investing:
Savings Bond Advisor, Tom Adams

David Scott's Guide to Investing in Bonds, David L Scott

For general investing, wealth accumulations:
DEAL with Your DEBT, Liz Pulliam Weston

The Millionaire Next Door, Thomas J. Stanley, Ph.D. and William D. Danko, Ph.D.

Raising Financially Fit Kids, Joline Godfrey

Let's Talk Money, James A. Barry, JR, CFP

Master Your Money, Ron Blue and Jeremy White, Foreword by Charles R. Swindoll

I Haven't Saved a Dime, Now What?! , Barbara Loos

Inspirational:
Last one, but a favorite of mine. This is a must read.
The Secret, by Rhonda Byrne. The author explains with simplicity the law that is governing all lives, and offers knowledge about how to create — intentionally and effortlessly — a joyful life. Available as a book, movie or audio CD.

Always check with your professional, legal, CPA and financial advisors before investing and taking tax deductions, since many of these topics are time sensitive.

ACKNOWLEDGMENTS

I thank my wife, Rose Brady, and my children, Jahana and Christina, for their support. And I thank my staff, Anita Knese, Mitzi Rogers, Cheryl Morton, Torrie Booher and Annette Liddicote, who helped in editing, especially for their help in ensuring the book was written in plain English, because English is a second language for me.

Thanks as well to Dwight Wheelan, Scott O'Brien and Scott Sidesinger.

Special thanks to my daughters, Jahana and Christina for their help in editing and illustration of this book.

John Azodi, CPA

August 13, 2009

ABOUT THE AUTHOR

John Azodi, CPA, is the owner and president of Azodi CPA & Investments, PC. He started his business in 1991 as a certified public accounting firm. In 1994, he expanded the business to provide 401(k) administration services to small and mid-size businesses. And in 1998, he expanded his services to include investments and insurance planning. He has taught a variety of seminars and classes on such topics as tax planning, starting and running a profitable business, and investment and retirement planning.

In 1974, at the age of 18, with limited knowledge of English, John moved from Iran to the United States where he put himself through college, graduating from the University of Colorado in 1982 with a Bachelor of Science degree in Accounting. He spent seven years in public accounting and two years as an office manager and controller for a physical rehabilitation agency before starting his own business. This is his first book.

As of the date of this publication, John Azodi, CPA, uses Berthel Fisher & Company Financial Services, Inc. as his broker/dealer.

Registered representative of and securities offered through Berthel Fisher & Company Financial Services, Inc., member FINRA/SIPC. Azodi CPA & Investments, PC is independent of and not associated with Berthel Fisher & Company Financial Services, Inc.

For additional copies of *Roth IRA Exploding the Myths*, please complete and fax to 816-455-9105

Or order on line at:
WWW.WhyRothIRA.Com Or at **www.Amazon.com**
Or https://www.createspace.com/3388745 or call 800-436-6571 or 816-455-9103.
Order Information:

Name _____

Company _____

Address _____

City _____ State ____ Zip _____

Phone _____ Fax _____

E-mail _____

QTY	Price	Shipping & Handling	Total	Total amount
	$19.00	$6.00	$25.00	
Discount: 5 to 49 books 10%				
Discount: 50 or more books 20%				
Net after quantity discount				

Make check payable to John Azodi, CPA
Or charge ____ MasterCard ____ Visa

Card # _____ Code _____

Expiration date _____ Name on Card _____

Signature _____

See next page if bought as gift

99

For an additional copy of **Roth IRA: Exploding the Myths** to be sent to a *friend or a student*, please complete this form and fax it to 816-455-9105, or call 800-436-6571 or 816-455-9103 or go to **WWW.WhyRothIRA.Com**

Name _____

Address _____

City _____ State _____ Zip _____

Phone _____ Fax _____

E-mail _____

Make check payable to John Azodi, CPA
Or charge _____ MasterCard _____ Visa

Card # _____ Code _____

Expiration date _____ Name on Card _____

Signature _____

Cost per book including shipping would be $20.00

_____ High School _____ College, Graduation Date _____

_____Include a letter from the author to the _____ graduate
Or _____ Friend _____ others _____

Name _____

Address _____

100

3923976

Made in the USA
Lexington, KY
06 December 2009